max fax

BIG CATS

Max Fax:

BIG CATS

Also in this series:
Cars
Sharks
Space

Cover photograph: A tiger

Series Concept: Dereen Taylor
Commissioning editor: Lisa Edwards
Series editor: Cath Senker
Designer: Luke Herriott
Language consultant: Wendy Cooling
Subject consultant: Stephen Savage
Picture researcher: Gina Brown
Illustrator: Mike Atkinson

Published in Great Britain in 2001 by Hodder Wayland,
an imprint of Hodder Children's Books
© Hodder Wayland 2001

The right of Claire Llewellyn to be identified as the author and Steve Roberts as the illustrator of this Work has been asserted by them in accordance with the Copyright, Designs and Patents Act 1988

All rights reserved. No part of this publication may be reproduced, stored in a retrieval system, or transmitted, in any form or by any means without the prior permission of the publisher, nor be otherwise circulated in any form of binding or cover other than that in which it is published and without a similar condition being imposed on the subsequent purchaser.

British Library Cataloguing in Publication Data
Llewellyn, Claire
Big Cats. – (Max Fax)
1. Panthera – Juvenile literature
I. Title
599.7'55

ISBN: 0 7502 3205 6
Printed and bound in Grafiasa, Porto, Portugal

Hodder Children's Books
A division of Hodder Headline Ltd
338 Euston Road, London NW1 3BH

BIG CATS

Claire Llewellyn

Hodder
Wayland

an imprint of Hodder Children's Books

CONTENTS

TOP CAT	8
BODY OF A HUNTER	10
ON THE MOVE	12
SILENT STALKER	14
FAMILY CAT	16
BRINGING UP BABY	18
CATS IN TROUBLE	20
CATS IN CAPTIVITY	22
MAN-EATERS	24
BIG CATS QUIZ	26
GLOSSARY	28
FINDING OUT MORE	29
INDEX	30

TOP CAT

Big cats are magnificent animals. They look good, and they move well. Like many creatures with a taste for meat, they have powerful claws, jaws and teeth.

Tigers, lions, cheetahs, jaguars and leopards are known as big cats. Big cats kill other animals for food, but are not hunted themselves. Big cats are at the top of the food chain.

The big cats are part of the cat family. There are small cats, too, such as the bobcat, lynx and puma – and the friendly pet cat at home.

The Siberian tiger can survive in freezing temperatures.

The puma is the largest of the small cats.

The snow leopard lives in the Himalayas. It can climb icy slopes and leap over rocky ravines.

Cats live in most parts of the world, except Australia and Antarctica. They live in forests, grasslands, mountains and deserts.

HOW MANY KINDS OF CAT ARE THERE?
There are 35 kinds of cat. The smallest is the pet cat. The biggest is the tiger.

HOW DO CATS COPE IN THE COLD?
They have thick coats, and huge furry paws that stop them sinking in the snow.

ARE PET CATS RELATED TO LIONS?
Yes. They belong to the same animal family – the *Felidae*.

The black leopard is also called a panther.

Big cats stay in their own territory, and roar to keep others away. Leopards, lions, tigers and jaguars can all roar loudly. But cheetahs can't roar, and nor can any of the small cats.

Body of a Hunter

Flexible backbone
A bendy backbone makes a cat really agile. It can move in many different ways.

A strong, sleek body, golden eyes and a fabulous coat of fur. Big cats are beautiful – but they are also deadly. Their bodies are designed to kill.

Tail
A long tail helps a cat to keep its balance as it runs, jumps and climbs trees.

A cat's padded paws help it to move silently. In between the pads are long, hooked claws that shoot out when the cat attacks.

Close-up of a lion's paw.

Paws
Huge paws and sharp claws deliver a powerful blow.

Whiskers
Long whiskers help a cat to touch and feel.

Eyes
A cat's eyes are close together on the front of its head. This helps it to judge distances well. Cats can also see in the dark.

A cat's longest, sharpest teeth are called its fangs. This tiger's fangs are 9 cm long – about as long as your middle finger.

Nose
A cat's nose picks up scents in the air. Cats have a good sense of smell.

Teeth
The large teeth stab, tear and slice meat.

Tongue
The tongue is covered with tiny spikes. These are good for scraping the meat off bones and for cleaning the cat's fur.

Jaws
The jaws are very strong, so the cat has a powerful bite.

Coat
A cat's coat makes great camouflage. A tiger's stripes blend in with grasses and trees, and keep the cat hidden from its prey.

Legs
Long, strong legs help cats to move fast and leap on to their prey.

DID YOU KNOW?

* A tiger's claws measure 10 cm. They help it to grip its prey.

* All leopards have their own pattern of spots, just as people have their own set of fingerprints.

* A large Siberian tiger weighs up to 384 kg – as much as four heavyweight boxers.

ON THE MOVE

The fastest animal on four legs is a cat. The cheetah is faster than the world's top racehorse. It reaches speeds of 95 kph. Some cats are great climbers and swimmers, too.

A leopard guards its kill.

Cheetahs attack herds of impalas and gazelles. Both these animals can run very fast, but a cheetah's speed gives it the edge. However, it can only sprint over short distances. If it doesn't catch its prey within 20 seconds, it will give up the chase.

Leopards spend a lot of time in the trees. They climb up by digging their claws into the trunk. They will even drag up their kill with them to stop other animals from stealing their meal.

A cheetah running

1. The cheetah pushes down with its back feet.

2. This powers the animal forwards.

Jaguars are quite at home in a river.

Some big cats love water. Jaguars often hunt in rivers for turtles, fish and even crocodiles. Tigers like water, too. They often wade into rivers to cool off or to hide from their prey.

DID YOU KNOW?

✸ Cheetahs can't pull in their claws. They use them like running spikes to grip the ground.

✸ Snow leopards can leap over an eight-metre-wide ravine – that's wider than a football goal.

✸ A cheetah can reach half its top speed from a standing start in just three seconds.

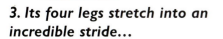

3. Its four legs stretch into an incredible stride…

4. …before its front feet hit the ground.

SILENT STALKER

Deadly bite: a leopard squeezes an impala's windpipe.

A cat has to kill every meal it eats. It creeps through the grass, with its eyes on its prey. Then it charges and leaps for the throat.

Big cats hunt many kinds of animals, from rabbits and small birds to large prey such as antelope, zebra and buffalo.

Big cats like to kill their prey quickly, before it has time to fight back. They fasten their teeth on its windpipe and squeeze tightly until the animal suffocates.

Most big cats hunt at dusk or at night, when it is cool and they won't be seen. They avoid hunting in bright moonlight.

CAT WATCH

'Our ears picked up the chase – hoofs smashing into the wet earth as zebras fled for their lives. At last came the sounds we were straining to hear – a thud and a wheeze as a lion slammed into a zebra, knocking the wind out of it as it fell.'

Dereck Joubert, National Geographic, Aug. 1994

A tiger attacks a deer

1. A hungry tiger hides in the long grass.

2. It creeps forward – freezes – then moves again.

3. Suddenly, it leaps and goes for the kill.

DID YOU KNOW?

* Bengal tigers can eat 31 kg of meat in one night – that's as much as 100 steaks.
* Lions make a successful kill in only one of every four attempts.
* Big cats don't compete with each other for food. They keep to their own territory.

A fishing cat catches its supper.

Fishing cats, which are small cats, enjoy a meal of fresh fish. They watch fish swimming in the water, then flip them out with their paws.

Family Cat

A pride of lions hunts together, feeds together, and raises its cubs together. Lions are the only cats to live in family groups. Most big cats live alone.

The lionesses (female lions) do most of the hunting for the pride. They stick together, growling softly to keep in touch.

After a kill, the pride members take it in turns to eat. The males eat first, the females eat second and any cubs eat last. The cubs get such poor scraps that many of them weaken and die.

Lionesses stand guard over their kill.

DID YOU KNOW?

✸ A bushy mane makes a lion look bigger and scares away rival males.

✸ About 10,000 years ago, there were lions living in Europe.

✸ Lions (and also tigers) can kill animals larger than themselves.

Lions wash one another. This spreads their scent so that all pride members smell the same.

Female cubs stay in the same pride all their lives, so they are usually all related. Sisters, aunts, nieces and cousins all help with each other's cubs. They will even suckle them if they have milk.

HOW BIG IS A PRIDE OF LIONS?
About 15 animals – one or two males, five or six females and a handful of youngsters and cubs.

WHAT DO LIONS DO WHEN THEY'RE NOT HUNTING?
They spend most of the time sleeping, sometimes as much as 18 hours a day!

DO ALL LIONS LIVE IN AFRICA?
No. About 300 lions live in India. They are called Asian lions.

Male lions defend a pride's territory by spraying its borders with urine, roaring loudly at dawn and dusk, and attacking other lions who dare to appear.

Lions have a deafening roar. In the still of the night, they may be heard about 8 km away.

Bringing up Baby

Lioness carrying her cub.

A litter of cubs lies hidden in the grass. Their mother hunts for food. The cubs grow quickly. Soon they will learn how to jump and stalk. Then they will learn how to kill.

A female cat keeps her cubs well hidden. From time to time, she will move them to a new hiding place. She picks them up gently with her teeth, grasping the loose fold of skin at the back of the neck.

Cubs love to play-fight with one another. The games help the cubs not only to grow stronger and react more quickly, but also to learn when to stop!

Cubs play-fight to practise hunting skills.

CAT WATCH

'It took me a moment to spot the three cubs lying on a little rock shelf…The two females dozed, but their brother was up and alert…His bright eyes focused on his mother far below, waiting for her signal to clamber down the hill and eat.'

Geoffrey C. Ward, National Geographic, Dec. 1997

Many cubs fail to survive. Some are poorly fed. Others are killed by hyenas, snakes – such as cobras – or other big cats.

Bringing up jaguar cubs

1. Jaguar cubs are born blind and helpless.

2. They feed on their mother's milk.

3. Later, she brings them meat.

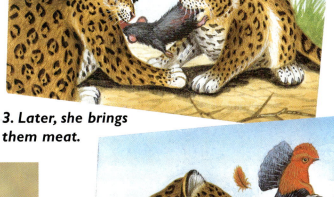

4. In time, they learn to hunt for themselves.

Most female cats bring up cubs alone. They have to kill enough food to feed both themselves and their cubs.

A cheetah with her cubs.

HOW MANY CUBS DO BIG CATS HAVE?
Most cats have two to four cubs.

WHY DO MALE LIONS SOMETIMES KILL YOUNG CUBS?
When a male lion beats a rival, it usually kills that lion's cubs.

WHEN DO CUBS LEAVE THEIR MOTHER?
When they are two to three years old, or sooner if she has another litter.

Cats in Trouble

Life isn't easy for big cats. Their numbers in the wild are falling. Their habitats are shrinking. Big cats are shot at by farmers. They are hunted for their bones and fur.

Many big cats live in forests, but the forests are shrinking fast. So each cat's territory is growing smaller and there is less prey for it to hunt.

Big cats have always been killed for their fur. The skins are made into rugs and coats, and sold all over the world. Most countries have tough laws to ban hunting, but there is still plenty of poaching.

Dead meat: a shop in Zimbabwe sells stuffed lion heads.

A drugged lion is fitted with a radio collar.

DID YOU KNOW?

* In the past, people caught and trained cheetahs to hunt for them.
* Tigers are killed for their bones. In traditional Chinese medicine, it is thought that the bones have special powers.
* There are around 5,000 Bengal tigers left in the wild.

Conservationists work to protect big cats. Sometimes they fit them with collars that give out radio signals. By following the signals, the scientists track the cats, and learn more about how they behave.

Tourism is helping to save big cats. Countries with wildlife reserves can earn huge sums of money each year from the thousands of tourists who go on safari.

Tourists watch cheetahs in a wildlife reserve in South Africa.

Cats in Captivity

Thousands of cats spend their lives in captivity. Some of them are in zoos. Others are in people's homes. And many end up in sanctuaries when there is nowhere else to go.

The best zoos do not have cages or bars.

WHY DO ZOO CATS OFTEN PACE UP AND DOWN?
Pacing may mean that the cat is bored or hungry.

DO BIG CATS LIVE LONGER IN ZOOS?
Yes. They can live for 20 years in zoos. In the wild, big cats live for up to 15 years.

HOW DO ZOOS FIND MATES FOR THEIR CATS?
They swap animals with other zoos around the world.

Good zoos make sure that big cats have indoor dens for breeding and outdoor space with grass and trees. Food is dragged around the enclosure to make a scent trail so that the cats have to look for their food.

Lions and tigers breed well in captivity. The best zoos breed them for conservation. Some day the young may be returned to the wild, if their habitat is still there and there is no danger of hunting.

CAT WATCH

'The Sheriff's Department contacted us about a puma. Susie had been discovered in an old chicken coop. She had been tied to a 60-cm chain for six years. It was very moving for us to watch her jump, eat grass, even learn how to walk straight – all for the first time.'

From the website of Wild About Cats, a sanctuary in California, USA

When a female cat is killed by poachers, she often leaves cubs behind. Many of them die, but some are found by wardens. They raise the cubs in sanctuaries and return them to the wild.

Some people keep big cats as pets, but in many cases, the 'pets' are turned out when they grow too big and wild.

KEY TO PICTURE
1. Resting place
2. Pool to swim in
3. Den
4. Tyre to play with
5. Tree for climbing
6. Wire mesh
7. Solid wooden wall
8. Double door

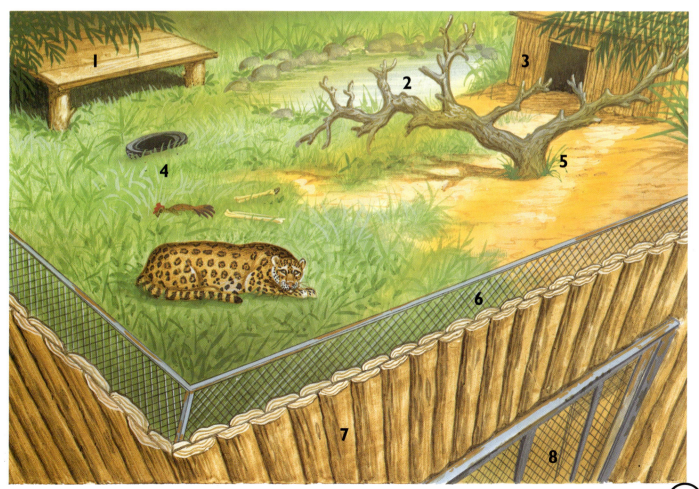

Rescued from poachers: sanctuaries do a useful job caring for homeless cats.

Man-Eaters

Big cats rarely attack humans. Most of them run away from people. But now and again, there are savage attacks. What makes cats behave like this? Why do they turn into man-eaters?

Training tigers in a circus is not natural. Occasionally, they may attack.

DID YOU KNOW?

* 2,000 years ago, the Romans enjoyed watching slaves being thrown to the lions.

* A female cat may attack a person who gets too close to her cubs.

* Taming takes time. Small cats have been living with people for over 5,000 years.

A cat in a circus sometimes attacks the trainer it has known all its life. Cats are wild animals. They can be trained but never tamed. If you turn your back on a big cat, it may attack.

Some big cats become man-eaters when they are too old, too wounded or too sick to hunt. Attacks like this are very serious, but rare.

Attacks can happen in zoos. This man was pushed into a lion's den. The lion attacked him.

A tiger attacks…

A big cat may attack a person if it is starving. This sometimes happens when people are working inside its territory, and scaring away its prey.

CAT WATCH

'A tiger pounced on a villager, but the man fought back and survived. Mahat Awang was checking a trap for wild boars on Saturday when the tiger leapt out of the bushes. He was bitten on his hands and the back of his head, and needed 50 stitches.'

Associated Press, 18 Jan. 1999

Big Cats Quiz

Can you find the right answers to these questions? They can all be found somewhere in this book. Check your answers on page 29.

1. How many kinds of big cat are there?
   a 5
   b 12
   c 35

2. Where does the snow leopard live?
   a In the Himalayas
   b In the Arctic
   c In all mountain areas

3. Which of the big cats cannot roar?
   a The leopard
   b The jaguar
   c The cheetah

4. What use is a big cat's tail?
   a It helps the cat to balance
   b It warns away enemies
   c It helps the cat to run faster

5. Which is the world's biggest cat?
   a The snow leopard
   b The tiger
   c The lion

6. Why do cats have padded paws?
   a To protect their claws
   b To stroke their cubs
   c To move quietly

7. What is a cheetah's top speed?
   a 9.5 kph
   b 95 kph
   c 195 kph

8. Which of these do jaguars like to eat?
   a Termites
   b Chimpanzees
   c Turtles

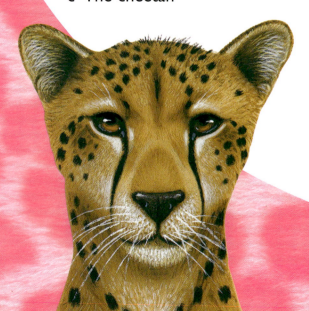

9. Why do big cats keep to their own territory?
a To avoid competing for food
b Because they prefer to live alone
c Because the forest is so small

10. Which cat cannot pull in its claws?
a The cheetah
b The leopard
c The tiger

11. How do big cats kill their prey?
a They drown it
b They shake it from side to side
c They suffocate it

12. How does a female cat carry her young?
a In a pouch
b In her mouth
c On her back

13. After a kill, which lions eat first?
a The females
b The cubs
c The males

14. How are tourists helping big cats?
a They spot poachers
b They bring in a lot of money
c They adopt motherless cubs

15. How long do big cats live in the wild?
a 5 years
b 15 years
c 50 years

16. How many Bengal tigers are left in the wild?
a About 1,000
b About 5,000
c About 500,000

17. Which parts of a tiger are used in traditional Chinese medicine?
a Its skin
b Its liver
c Its bones

18. How is a man-eater likely to attack?
a From behind
b From above
c In water

GLOSSARY

agile Quick-moving and active.

camouflage The colours and markings on a cat's fur, which help it to blend in with its surroundings and make it difficult to see.

captivity Being imprisoned and kept in a cage.

conservation Keeping the environment, including wild animals, safe from harm.

conservationist A person who wants to protect wildlife and help it to survive.

enclosure A piece of land that is surrounded by a fence or wall.

food chain A food chain shows the feeding links between living things. Each link in the food chain feeds on the one below it. For example, lions eat zebras, which feed on grass.

gazelle A type of antelope.

habitat The type of place where an animal usually lives; for example, a pond, river or forest.

impala A type of antelope.

poaching Catching animals that are protected by law.

prey Animals that are hunted by others for food.

pride A group of lions that live together.

safari A trip to see African animals in the wild.

sanctuary A safe place where homeless cats are cared for until a new home can be found for them.

territory The piece of land where a big cat hunts for food, and which it will defend against other big cats.

urine A waste liquid made inside the body. It is yellow and has a strong smell.

wardens Keepers in sanctuaries or zoos, who look after the animals.

wildlife reserve A piece of land that has been set aside for the protection of wild animals.

windpipe The air tube that lies between the throat and the lungs.

FINDING OUT MORE

Books
The African Cats by Geoffrey C. Saign (Watts, 1999)

Big Cat Conservation by Peggy Thomas (Twenty-First Century Books, 2000)

Eyewitness Guides: Cat by Juliet Clutton-Brock (Dorling Kindersley, 1991)

I Didn't Know That Only Some Big Cats Can Roar And Other Amazing Facts About Wild Cats by Claire Llewellyn (Aladdin/Watts, 1999)

Natural World: Lion by Bill Jordan (Wayland, 1999)

Natural World: Tiger by Valmik Thapar (Wayland, 1999)

Wild Cats of the World by David Alderton (Cassell, 1993)

Video
Eyewitness: Cat (Dorling Kindersley, 1994)

Websites
http://dialspace.dial.pipex.com/agarman
www.bigcats.com
www.bornfree.org.uk (website of the Born Free Foundation)
www.midcoastmaine.com/bjh/depart/curric/animals
www.wildaboutcats.org
www.wwf-uk.org (website of WWF-UK)

Places to visit
You can see big cats at zoos in the following places: Bristol, Chester, Colchester, Edinburgh, Glasgow, Howletts and Port Lympne in Kent, London, Marwell, Paignton, Whipsnade and Woburn.

Answers to quiz

1	a	7	b	13	c
2	a	8	c	14	b
3	c	9	a	15	b
4	a	10	a	16	b
5	b	11	c	17	c
6	c	12	b	18	a

INDEX

Page numbers in **bold** mean there is a picture on the page.

A
attack, lion 17, 25
attack, tiger **15**, 24, 25, **25**

B
body 10, **10**, 11, **11**
breeding 22

C
cats, types of 8, **8**, 9, **9**
cheetah 9, 12, **12**, 13, **13**, 19, 21, **21**
circuses 24, **24**
claws 10, 11
coat 9, **11**
conservationists 21, **21**
cubs 16, 17, 18, **18**, 19, **19**, 23

D
dens 22, 23, **23**

E
enclosures 22, **22**, 23

F
fishing cat 15, **15**

H
hunting (by big cats) 13, 14, **15**, 16, 18, 19
hunting (of big cats) 20

J
jaguar 13, **13**, 19, **19**, 23

L
leopard 9, 11, 12, **12**, 14
lion 9, 14, 15, 16, **16**, 17, **17**, 18, 19, 20, 21, 22, 25
lioness 16, **16**, 17, 18

M
mane 16, **17**
man-eaters 24, 25

P
pacing 22
paws 9, 10, **10**

play-fighting 18, **18**
poaching 20, 23
puma **8**, 23

R
roaring 9, 17, **17**

S
sanctuaries 22, 23, **23**
snow leopard **9**, 13

T
tail 10, **10**
teeth 11, **11**, 14, 18
tiger 8, **10**, **11**, 13, 15, **15**, 21, 22, **22**, 24, **24**, 25, **25**
tourism 21, **21**

W
washing **17**
wildlife reserves 21, **21**

Z
zoos 22, **22**, 25

Picture acknowledgements

Bruce Coleman 9 (below), (HPH Photography) 21 (below), 24; Getty Images (Mark Petersen) 16, (Kevin Shafer) 18 (above), (Manoj Shah) 19; NHPA (Andy Rouse) Cover, (Kevin Shafer) 8 (above), (Andy Rouse) 8 (below), (John Shaw) 12, (Jamy Sauvanet) 13, (Nigel Dennis) 17 (above), (Christophe Ratier) 21 (above); OSF (Frank Schneidermever) 18 (below); Panos (David Reed) 20; Popperfoto 25; RSPCA (Klaus-Peter Wolf) 22; Still Pictures (Klein/Hubert) 9 (above), (Fritz Polking) 10, (Michel Gunther) 11, M. & C. Denis-Huot 14, (Roland Seitre) 15, (Muriel Nicolotti) 17 (below).